EASY AND EFFECTIVE MARKETING TOOLS FOR BUILDING A PROSPEROUS LAW PRACTICE

Become a Rainmaker and Get Known as an Expert!

EASY AND EFFECTIVE MARKETING TOOLS
FOR BUILDING A PROSPEROUS LAW PRACTICE
Become a Rainmaker and Get Known as an Expert!

ISBN: 978-1501077814

EASY AND EFFECTIVE
MARKETING TOOLS FOR BUILDING A **PROSPEROUS LAW PRACTICE**

Proven Rainmaking Advice from Leading Experts as Well as Tips and Techniques for Positioning Yourself as an Expert

Terri Levine & Judy Weintraub

TABLE OF **CONTENTS**

PREFACE

Dear Counselor,

You may wonder why you struggle to find new clients, and whether the pressure of being a Rainmaker is ever going to go away or if it's going to wear you down.

You may also wonder how you are supposed to find the time to work with your current clients effectively when you also need time to go hunt for new prospective clients.

If you are asking yourself these or similar questions, then this book is written for you. We know that attorneys have difficulties and struggle with these questions. How do we know? Judy is an attorney. Terri is a business mentor to attorneys. We also know from our experience that there are solutions that work and produce great results for attorneys.

Attorneys typically are not effective rainmakers. Marketing is not a natural skill and is not taught in law schools or in CLE courses. We can show you how to obtain status as a credible expert which will give you a great way to attract clients and get you more of the results you are seeking with your marketing in a lot less time.

We don't expect that this book will turn you into good marketers. Rather, our aim is to help you get known as the expert you are and to show you some easy, inexpensive means for growing your clientele.

We have helped thousands of people just like you achieve their goals of creating a financially successful and personally satisfying practice. In this book you will discover several principles and tools you can use to become the credible expert in your area of law.

As you embark on this journey with us, be prepared to take a lot of notes. We are going to give you specific concrete strategies that when applied will make a dramatic difference in your law practice today, tomorrow and forever.

We are excited to help you improve your law practice and your life.

Terri Levine,
The Business Mentoring Expert

Judy Weintraub,
Esq., CEO of SkillBites LLC

INTRODUCTION

Today's legal landscape is filled with rough terrain. With the prevalence of information and forms on the internet, many people serve as their own legal counsel, without any legal training. Businesses that have been hard hit by the economic downturn are forcing law firms to reduce their billable rates. Law firms are not hiring or are downsizing, yet law schools continue to turn out large numbers of graduates.

Gone are the days when a lawyer could put out a shingle and, with a bit of expertise, run a lucrative practice. To be successful today, lawyers need to run their practice more like a business. They need to develop effective systems, understand financials and continuously market themselves to build a sustainable practice, all while performing legal services for their existing clients. Not an easy task.

In this book, we focus on the marketing issue, as without effective marketing, even the best run firm will not survive very long. We approach marketing from

two angles: becoming a rainmaker and positioning oneself as an expert. Obviously, law firms need clients, and rainmakers are the ones who bring clients in to the firm. We define a rainmaker as someone who generates significant new business through relationship-based marketing.

To be an effective rainmaker requires, among other things, being able to promote and sell one's services. Yet most attorneys feel uncomfortable in that role. Fortunately, these skills can be learned. We describe a four step process and provide many tools and techniques to enable attorneys to improve their marketing skills and their relationship-building skills so they can become better rainmakers and build profitable law practices.

We don't stop there, however. We delve into another powerful approach for attorneys to market themselves called content marketing. Content marketing consists of providing information that demonstrates that the creator knows the subject matter and that provides value to the audience. The attorney who produces information products thereby positions himself or herself as an expert and gains the appreciation of the recipient who benefits from the information. Such information products significantly enhance the attorney's credibility and visibility, leading more people to retain him or her. We provide a number of tips for producing effective content marketing and discuss ten types of information products, as well as some of their pros and cons.

We know that most attorneys would prefer to focus on the practice of law, and not on the business of building a legal practice. We have kept this book short so it won't take long to get through, and we have stocked it with easy, effective and economical techniques to help you grow your practice quickly. We hope you find it useful.

RAINMAKING

No law fim can survive without rainmaking. In this section we cover what this means and how to become a rainmaker.

WHAT IS A RAINMAKER?

A rainmaker is an attorney who can generate a great deal of business for themselves and their firm through relationship-based marketing. By using their contacts in the community rainmakers continuously network, seek to expand their networks and bring clients to the firm. Rainmakers create the practice they want as well as the sustainable income they desire.

WHAT ARE THE QUALITIES OF A SUCCESSFUL RAINMAKER?

The attorneys who are masters of rainmaking all share some common traits. They are self-confident and well known in their communities because they are actively engaged in community organizations and associations. They clearly understand their ideal target audience and all have stellar "Core Unique Positioning Statements." They know how to use those statements and have integrated them into all of their marketing.

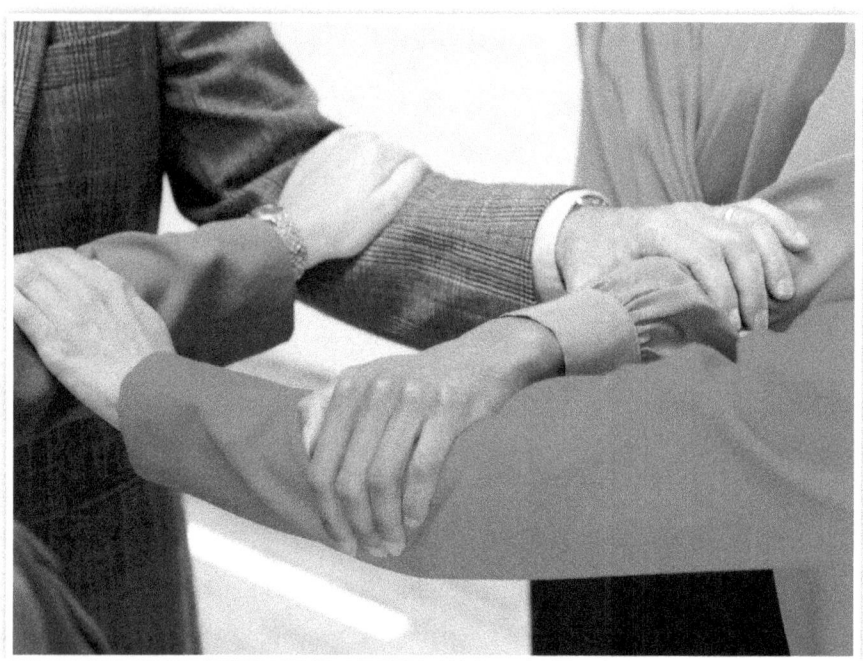

HOW TO BECOME A RAINMAKER

Becoming a rainmaker consists of 4 steps. These are:

1. Identify your target market
2. Develop your Core Unique Positioning Statement
3. Build relationships
4. Use Guerrilla Marketing tactics

Once you have mastered these 4 steps you are ready to make it rain!

Step 1:
Identify Your Target Market

One of the biggest mistakes attorneys make in marketing is that they begin marketing without first identifying who their ideal clients are. So they end up spending valuable (billable) time targeting "everyone".

The first step to market a legal practice successfully is to identify who your ideal target client is. You must know the demographic and psychographic information about the clients you want to work with. Demographic characteristics include age, occupation, income level, education and other objective factors. Psychographic traits, less objective but equally relevant, include personality traits, attitudes, values and lifestyle choices.

For your legal practice to succeed, it must have enough clients regularly hiring your attorneys. Be certain you have invested the time to evaluate your potential client base and are certain you're targeting the right client audience.

Your ideal target customers are those most likely in need of the legal services your firm offers who are ready to hire a firm like yours. Once you identify this audience, with great specificity, then you can tailor your marketing efforts, and your legal services, to those clients.

Don't get concerned that you will limit your firm's abilities to attract clients. Having a very specific and defined target market actually increases your marketing efficiency and allows you to focus your marketing efforts on potential clients who you have determined are likely to use your legal services -- rather than wasting time and money courting the vast world of prospects who merely could become clients. This is a much more effective approach.

Create a Client Profile

Defining your ideal target market means identifying the specific characteristics of the people or businesses who you believe are most likely to buy your legal services. The set of characteristics or traits is sometimes referred to as a demographic profile. Common characteristics used to classify clients include:

- ❏ age
- ❏ gender
- ❏ income level
- ❏ buying habits
- ❏ occupation or industry
- ❏ marital status
- ❏ family status
- ❏ geographic location
- ❏ ethnic group
- ❏ political affiliations
- ❏ hobbies and interests.

Be certain that you are very specific when you are creating your ideal client profile. The more narrowly you've defined your target market, the more likely your marketing efforts will pay off. When you have fully completed this step, you are ready for step 2.

Step 2:
Develop Your Core Unique
Positioning Statement

The second step in developing an effective marketing strategy is to develop a "CUPS". The Core Unique Positioning Statement (CUPS) is the key message communicated across your website, branding, letterhead, business cards, blog, social media, advertising, and so on; or at least it should be. As you know, there are unique reasons a customer should choose you over a competitor, but are you spreading that message so your target audience is aware of it? Perhaps you do something for free or at a low cost, offer a comprehensive guarantee on your work, or have a progressive financing policy. Whatever it is that makes you the clear choice, you need to create messaging that reflects that reason in an equally-clear voice.

The Two Key Questions

Discovering or creating your firm's Core Unique Positioning Statement begins with you answering two key questions:

1. Why do people choose your firm?

2. If they aren't choosing your firm now, why should they?

A law firm today must have some kind of a sustainable competitive advantage. This is what sets it apart from the competition or makes it unique. In today's highly competitive marketplace however, it is often difficult to determine what is unique about a particular legal practice. Many times there is nothing unique about it. In that case, the firm must establish something that it offers that the competition does not offer that creates extra value or gives people an additional reason to hire that firm.

Types of Core Unique Positioning Statements

The Core Unique Positioning Statement competitive advantage can take form in several different ways. For example:

1. The firm can be the price leader. This means that out of all the competitors in the market, the firm charges the lowest fees. This is a great advantage if it can be created and maintained. However, it is often difficult to consistently be the price leaders.

    An example of a CUPS for a firm that is a price leader might be: "Quality professional attorneys at fees you can afford."

2. The firm can differentiate itself by offering a unique service. This means that the firm creates an advantage by doing something more or better or different than the competition. It could be in the form of longer hours, better guarantee, higher quality, more selection, etc.

    An example of a CUPS for a firm that does something different is: "We are the one and only law firm to offer five complimentary hours of office time to field legal questions from Mainers about: motor vehicle accidents, personal injury, social security disability, medical malpractice and workers' compensation."

    Mainers – Natives or inhabitants of the state of Maine.

3. The firm can focus on a narrow niche. This means that they zero in on only one small vertical segment of the market and then become either the price leader or they differentiate themselves in some way, but only to that small segment of the market. An example of a CUPS for a firm that differentiates by segmentation is: "Morgan Sports Law LLP is a boutique law firm devoted to sports arbitration and litigation. Our lawyers are known in particular for their expertise in cases involving doping, corruption and eligibility disputes."

No matter which way you go to create your competitive advantage, it is crucial that your firm develop a distinct Core Unique Positioning Statement as the foundational message underlying all of your marketing.

Integrating Your Core Unique Positioning Statement

Once you have created a strong Core Unique Positioning Statement, the next step is to fully integrate this statement into everything that represents your business -- your website, stationery, business cards, invoices, receipts, email signature file, phone messages on hold, the way the phones are answered, voice mail messages, etc.

In order to accomplish this, all of your team must be trained on what your Core Unique Positioning Statement is and that it is not simply a statement. It is in fact the foundation from which you will be operating your business and making all your decisions. This point must be made clear so that staff understands that embracing this statement is part of their responsibility and one of your expectations.

Every staff member should have the Core Unique Positioning Statement memorized so that they can share it with clients and prospects, and so that prospects and clients know that they are making a great choice to hire your law firm. This is how you truly leverage and optimize your Core Unique Positioning Statement.

Once you have developed your CUPS and integrated it fully, you are ready for the 3rd step in the process.

Step 3:
Build Relationships

Now you have an effective message to share with others. Rainmaking comes from building relationships face-to-face and then ongoing communication after those relationships have been established.

Building relationships doesn't mean delivering your Core Unique Positioning Statement and handing out business cards. It means asking questions and being interested versus merely listening to people and their situations; and then saying, "If I can be of service let me know", and delivering your Core Unique Positioning Statement.

Let me give you an example. I was recently at an event in my community as a service volunteer where my ideal client audience was present (business owners such as attorneys, dentists, doctors, etc). As I met other volunteer workers I chatted with them and asked what they did, where their business was located and how their business was doing with the economic changes in our community. I listened as they talked, without any agenda of selling them anything. If (and only if) they inquired about what I did, did I deliver my Core Unique Positioning Statement, "I show business professionals who are struggling with filling their customer base how to use my Rapid ROI model to deliver all the leads they need in a way that doesn't overwhelm them or their business."

Think about organizations to join where your ideal target market may be - social, civic, etc. Join some of those. Develop relationships with key community members as well as other attorneys. By developing these attorney relationships you can generate cross referrals. Network with other professionals such as financial planners, accountants, and doctors, with whom you can develop cross referrals as well. By developing an extensive network, you can naturally and continuously generate business without constantly having to spend a lot of money or time hunting for clients.

Here is a list of possible audiences to cultivate. Depending on your area of practice, some of these may not be relevant, and there are likely others not on this list that would be beneficial for you to pursue.

- ❑ Past and current clients
- ❑ Other attorneys

- ❑ Advocates
- ❑ Referral partners (accountants, doctors, bankers, financial planners, etc.)
- ❑ Competitors
- ❑ Judges
- ❑ Alumni
- ❑ Arbitrators/Mediators
- ❑ Business Owners
- ❑ People in your civic, social, and academic groups
- ❑ Family members
- ❑ Friends
- ❑ People from your past

And now we move on to step 4!

Step 4:
Use Guerrilla Marketing Tactics

The basis of Guerrilla Marketing is to use low and no cost tactics to build your law firm. Considering what you learned about your ideal target audience and how that audience might desire to connect with you, pick some of these Guerrilla Marketing tactics and do them weekly to make it rain!

- ❑ Ask for referrals
- ❑ Ask referral sources to make an introduction (to their accountant, banker, advisors, etc)
- ❑ Send mail - personal letters, announcement letters, nice to meet you notes
- ❑ Make warm calls (call or arrange to meet someone you already know but have not received work from.)
- ❑ Serve on committees that interest you
- ❑ Serve on boards that interest you
- ❑ Serve as a volunteer for groups in which you are interested
- ❑ Become a sponsor of a group or organization
- ❑ Have an open house in your firm
- ❑ Be an active member of your State Bar Association
- ❑ Participate in industry associations
- ❑ Enroll in business groups
- ❑ Attend meetings and participate in community affairs
- ❑ Get involved with charitable organizations
- ❑ Join your chamber of commerce
- ❑ Become an active member of Rotary, Kiwanis or like-minded groups
- ❑ Take advantage of your involvement with your religious or spiritual organization

KEEP THE WATER FLOWING

Now that you have begun creating rain you must continue the relationships you have developed. Relationships need to be nurtured and deepened and this requires frequent and regularly scheduled actions on your part.

The following is a list of possible relationship building activities:

- ❑ Invite them for lunch or coffee
- ❑ Visit them in their office
- ❑ Find ways to get to know their business
- ❑ Send newspaper clippings or information that would interest them
- ❑ Send invitations to meetings or seminars
- ❑ Send newsletters
- ❑ Inform contacts of changes in the law that might affect them
- ❑ Send notes acknowledging their accomplishments
- ❑ Make referrals to your contacts
- ❑ Volunteer at your contact's events
- ❑ Send thank you and other cards, personalized letters and short notes
- ❑ Engage in entertainment activities like golf, dinner, sport events, theatre, or something in the neighborhood with your contacts
- ❑ Serve on your contact's committees

POSITIONING YOURSELF
AS AN EXPERT

If you practice law in a fairly large metropolitan area, then there are undoubtedly hundreds if not thousands of other lawyers in the same practice area in your region. As was discussed above, you need to find a way to differentiate yourself from those other lawyers. One of  the best ways to do that is to become known as an expert in your practice area. Not only will this elevate you above your competition, it will also help you get the word out about your practice and will increase your credibility.

Prospects become clients when they trust that you have the expertise to handle their problems.

When you position yourself as an expert in your subject matter, you earn that trust. Then those facing a problem in that area are more likely to retain you, and when they hear of others needing your expertise, they'll refer you. Moreover, when you are known for being an expert, you can command a higher fee.

A powerful strategy for becoming known as an expert is called content marketing – providing information that demonstrates that you know the subject matter and that provides value to the audience. Some of the common types of content marketing include writing a book, giving a speech, teaching a course, writing articles and blog posts, sending out a newsletter and appearing on TV. This chapter delves into several content marketing techniques.

PRELIMINARY CONSIDERATIONS

Before jumping into the techniques, though, it is important to start with some fundamentals. What do you want to be known for? Perhaps you have a broad practice, taking any case that comes along, or handling a number of diverse issues. While that may be appealing from the standpoint of variety, it doesn't tend to lead to a lucrative law practice. When you handle many different types of legal matters, you don't gain the in depth knowledge of any one area. We recommend picking one area and focusing on it as your area of specialty.

Next, think about how your ideal clients are likely to find out about you. Where do they go for legal referrals? Would they be more likely to look online or offline? Are they members of any particular industry association? What magazines do they read? This analysis will enable you get in front of them in the manner that would appeal to them, perhaps speaking at an industry association meeting, or writing articles for a trade journal, or submitting guest blog posts for blogs they read. Further, the more you know about your ideal clients, the better able you'll be to develop content that is valuable to and resonates with that audience, leading them to be more inclined to trust you and retain you when the need arises.

Regardless of which content marketing strategy you choose to utilize, here are some key tips to keep in mind:

1. **Choose a pertinent topic** – and the narrower the topic the better. The best topics are ones that solve a problem that your ideal client is facing. Chances are, people with that problem are looking online for a solution, so if you have an eBook, blog post or online article on the subject, your content will be found. To make sure your topic is pertinent, you can ask your customers or prospects whether they are interested in the subject, by running a survey, or asking questions on social media.

2. **Use a compelling title** – You want to pique your audience's interest. The best titles are short, convey the benefits and utilize key words that are being used to search for the particular topic. A few popular title formats

include "The Five Secrets to _____" or "The Top 7 Mistakes People Make When _____".

3. **Provide high quality** – If you are producing something in writing, make sure there are no typos or grammatical mistakes. If you are doing a live presentation, practice so that you can speak fluently, without umms and other distracting sounds. If you are doing a recorded presentation, make sure there is no background noise. You don't want anything to detract from the quality of the content you are providing.

4. **List the benefits** – Write out what the audience will gain from consuming your information. This will keep you focused on your message.

5. **Organize your thoughts** – Brainstorm all of the issues you want to cover. Put yourself in the shoes of your audience – what would they want to know? What obstacles might they stumble on? Then collate your ideas into categories, review the list to determine whether you want to eliminate any topics or save them for a different product, and then put them into a logical order. That will expedite your ability to produce the content.

6. **Develop a game plan** – Determine when you will have your product completed, and then figure out what you need to do to meet that deadline – e.g., work on it every day for 30 minutes, or perhaps Mondays and

Wednesdays from 8 – 9 am. You are more likely to stick to your goal and make progress if you are held accountable. Is there someone you can request to hold you accountable? Think about what could get in the way. Is there something you are currently doing that you could either eliminate or reduce the time you spend doing it (e.g., posting on Facebook or watching TV)? Is there any work or tasks you can delegate to free some time to work on the product?

7. ***Think about leveraging your product*** – How will you use the product to achieve your objectives? You may need to develop a campaign to follow up with each person who views or hears your content. That could require preparing a series of emails, or creating a script for telephone calls. Develop a plan so you know what actions to take and when.

TYPES OF INFORMATION PRODUCTS

Which type of information product should you choose? The answer to that depends in part on your audience, and in part on your own preference. Is your audience more likely to attend a live presentation or read an eBook or listen to a podcast? To determine this, you can ask them, or hire someone to do some market research for you. Are you more comfortable writing or speaking before a live audience, or recording a video presentation? You'll have a better idea of which way to proceed when you can answer those questions.

In this section, we will briefly discuss some of the pros and cons of the more popular types of information products.

Books

There is no better way to earn the trust of your prospects than to be a published author. When you publish a book, you are perceived as an expert. Being a published author enables you to generate more leads, close more deals, charge higher fees, and get better speaking engagements, to name just a few of the many benefits. In a study cited by *Forbes* and *BusinessWeek*, 96% of surveyed business authors "realize a significant positive impact on their businesses from writing a book and would recommend the practice."

One of the primary difficulties with writing a book is the time required to write, publish and promote the book. To minimize this issue, you may want to think about writing a series of short books, rather than one or more long books. Long books take longer to write, and, because they also take longer to read, it is less likely that the reader will actually read them. The average person gets through 18 pages of a non-fiction book before putting it down and not returning to it. So if you want the reader to read your book completely, you are better off writing a short book, say 20 – 30 pages, and putting your best wisdom in it. It will be quicker to write, less expensive to produce, easier to give out to people and more likely to be read. You can focus on a narrow topic that is important to your ideal client. In addition, you can write a series of short books so you become a serial author, which is more powerful than being an author of a single book; and later, if you desire, you can combine the short books into a long one.

Another alternative is having a ghostwriter write a book for you. Generally, the ghostwriter will conduct a few extensive interviews with you and then call or email with additional questions during the writing stage. You will have the opportunity to review the draft book and provide comments and revisions. Many people balk at the idea of having someone else write their content. You'd be surprised how many authors use ghostwriters. Ghostwriting has become widely accepted and utilized, and is much quicker and usually better quality than the author could write themselves. Make sure you have a work for hire clause that gives you copyright ownership of the book's content.

Another issue many attorneys have with writing books is not knowing where to start. We can help you with that, as we have written a book on how to write a book. You can download a complimentary copy of this eBook by visiting the webpage *www.skillbites.net/writeabook*. Once the book is written, we can also help get it published and provide assistance with leveraging the book to grow your practice.

Articles

Since articles are much shorter than books, they are easier and quicker to write. Industry association newsletters are frequently looking for good content, and you can find many online article sites to submit articles to, such as *ezinearticles.com* and *articlecity.com*. Once your article is published, you can (if the publisher allows) add the article to your website and send copies of the published articles to your prospects. You could also send your articles to important reporters and analysts that cover your industry, so they call on you when they need someone with your expertise to opine on a current issue.

Before writing an article for a journal, make sure you understand the parameters for the article, such as word length, scope, who owns the content, and whether the journal has exclusivity (that is, whether you are allowed to send the article to multiple sources). Judy, for instance, publishes regularly in *The Legal Intelligencer*. *The Legal Intelligencer* owns the copyright to the articles she writes and prohibits the articles from being submitted to other journals. Moreover, to send copies of the articles with *The Legal Intelligencer's* masthead to prospects requires payment of a fee to *The Legal Intelligencer*.

Blogs

Blogs are an increasingly popular means of sharing knowledge, building a reputation for being an expert and developing a following. When the blog is a part of a website, it also helps with the search engine optimization of the website and brings more traffic to the website. Blogs are typically 300 – 700 words, so they can be written quickly. Each time you post to your blog, you can put an update on social media, to drive people to view your blog post.

Blogs should have fresh content at least weekly, so don't start one unless you are willing to make an ongoing commitment. If you don't want to start your own, you can find blogs that your prospects read and submit guest blog posts to those blogs. You can also seek to submit posts to the blogs of well-known experts in your field, thereby associating your name with their name. Remember to include your contact information in your byline. If you do want to start a blog, there are several sites on the internet that offer free blog platforms, such as WordPress. For each blog post, you should include an image to make the page more appealing.

Social Media

There are many social media channels, with the three most popular being Facebook, LinkedIn and Twitter. First you need to determine which social media channels your target audience is spending time on and then you'll want to join groups on these communities. For instance, if your prospects tend to favor LinkedIn, you'll want to join LinkedIn groups that your clients and prospects are likely to have joined. Then offer advice to people who are asking questions in those groups, and respond to discussions posted in the group. If you are really the go-to expert in your field, your advice will rise above the advice that others give.

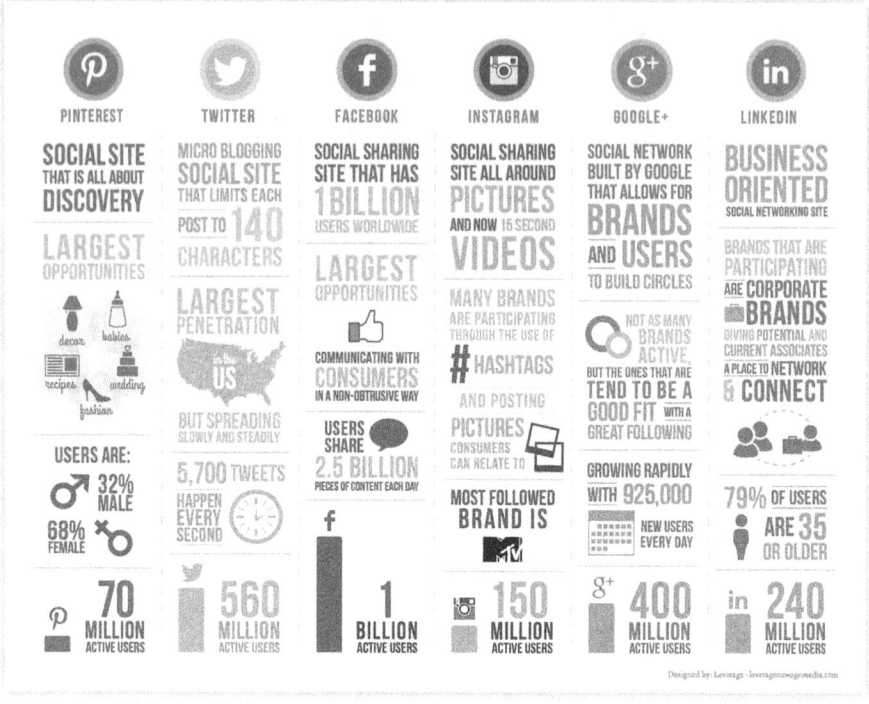

Look to join 2 or 3 groups that are large and active, and plan to add content at least on a weekly basis. When you are a frequent contributor, your name will gain recognition, causing people to read your content more. Group contributors have four times as many people read their profile.

Newsletters

Newsletters keep you in front of your prospects and customers, so when they need an attorney with your expertise, they are more likely to call you. Like blogs, however, newsletters are an ongoing commitment. Most newsletters come out at least monthly, if not more often, and it can be time consuming to create fresh content.

Newsletters can be in print or online. Print newsletters are more costly, and take a bit more time to send out; however, online newsletters are less likely to be read. Newsletters can be subscription based or free. Free newsletters are more likely to attract a wider audience, but the prospect who pays to receive your newsletter is more likely to hire you when the need arises.

Presentations

Presentations give you the opportunity to build a relationship with the audience in a way that books, articles and other written content does not offer. When  you give a presentation, you have a captive audience; and when people see you and hear you on stage, and enjoy your presentation, you gain their allegiance. Unlike the written information products, however, when you give a presentation your audience is confined to the people listening to you at that time. With books or articles, you can reach a much larger audience.

Look for the opportunity to speak at industry association meetings and conferences where your clientele are likely to be present. Associations are always looking for speakers. When you have been invited to give a presentation, let everyone know. Post the details on social media, and on your website and blog.

When giving a live presentation, don't make it a sales pitch. Make sure you provide a handout to the attendees, so they have something tangible from you and will have your contact information handy when they need it. Include in your presentation an enticing call to action, such as a free consultation or a significant discount off of a service or product you offer, to get people to retain you that day. Once they have left the venue, you stand less chance of converting them. Nevertheless, you should also develop a plan to follow up with the attendees who haven't taken advantage of your call to action.

Host Events

You can host a live conference or an internet webinar and be the moderator or the MC getting other experts on your topic (with the same clientele but from different fields) to speak. Use a service like *www.eventbrite.com*. It's interesting that as the host of such an event you become the most noticed person. You also get to speak and introduce yourself, deliver your Core Unique Positioning Statement and have people sign up for the event on a landing page you've built on the web, so you get all those contacts. You won't lack for new prospects and all those prospects will see you as the credible expert because YOU interviewed those big name guests.

Before hosting an online event, make sure you thoroughly understand and have tested the platform you are using. You don't want technical glitches to ruin your show. Similarly, when doing live events in person, confirm that the venue has been set up properly and any a/v equipment you'll need is available, is set up and works. Do you need a remote to operate your PowerPoint presentation? If so, bring extra batteries, just in case. Will your cord reach the outlet? Bring an extension cord, just in case.

Pitch the Press

Determine which radio and TV shows as well as print publications cover your field. Then, reach out to the appropriate people with a story idea that they may find of interest. The media is always looking for good content. You can agree with something the media has reported or even disagree.

Write editorials to your local papers and also offer to write a column for them. Share your expertise and advice and give tips, suggestions and information that the community and readers can really use and will appreciate.

There are some resources you can use to find reporters looking for stories in your field. For instance, *www.haro.com* (where haro stands for help a reporter out) has a daily list of topics on which reporters are looking for someone to provide expert opinions or advice.

Public Television

Here is a marketing idea that almost no attorneys think of. Almost every community in the United States has a public access television station with volunteer broadcast personnel, for anyone in the community to use. Create a 30 or 60-minute information-based and entertaining public access television show, offering solutions for your ideal clients' most common problems. Use FREE public access distribution channels to offer your show to public access channels globally that are hungry for good, quality video content. This can all be done for minimal cost. You may have to pay a fee to take a course that teaches you how to run the station's equipment, and you may want to pay a consultant to help you appear your best, but running the show won't cost you a dime.

We've given you a lot of ideas here and there are plenty more. Instead of doing them all, we suggest you pick one or two and put them into action. Put in place some measures that will allow you to evaluate whether they are working for you, and if not, determine whether you need to adjust how you are implementing them or switch to other ideas. Once you determine that the implementation is working, look for ways to systematize the work so you free yourself to take on additional content marketing strategies.

SUMMARY

Building a prosperous law practice requires developing a steady stream of clients. We have shared two approaches for developing this stream. The first half of the book addressed rainmaking. We provided a four step process for becoming an effective rainmaker. The first step is to identify your target market. Who is most in need of your services? Who do you most want to work with? Once you identify your target market, you will create a client profile, consisting of the key characteristics of that group.

The second step is to develop your Core Unique Positioning Statement or key message which explains why people should hire you. This message should be integrated into everything you do – your website, business cards, elevator speech, etc.

The third step is to build relationships with your community and members of your target market. You should join professional groups and boards, go to events, donate time to charities, speak at public events, give presentations and guest lectures, and make it seem like you are everywhere. The more you put your name out there and are seen, the more name recognition you earn along with critically important third party validation. Even if someone has never met you, you will have the backing of trusted sources that confirm your credibility as well as people saying, "I've heard of you." This goes a long way.

The fourth step is to implement Guerilla Marketing tactics to nurture the relationships you are building. We shared with you over 15 tactics, and recommend that you choose 2 or 3 of them, based on what you think your target market would desire. Do them often and consistently, and if one tactic isn't working for you, try a different one to try.

In the second half of the book, we focused on how to position yourself as an expert through content marketing. When you are seen as an expert, you will get more people choosing to hire you and referring you to others.

We provided a number of preliminary considerations that pertain to whichever strategy you choose to pursue, such as choosing a good topic and a compelling title, and making sure the product quality is sufficient. We then shared several options for getting known as an expert, from writing books, articles, newsletters and blogs to giving presentations and even getting on TV.

Once again, the decision of which strategy to pursue depends in part on the preference of your target market. That is why it is so important to identify that target market and the characteristics of your ideal client. You also want to consider your own predilections. Perhaps you don't feel comfortable speaking or appearing on TV, but enjoy writing. Then you'll want to focus more on the strategies that involve writing, and look for blogs, magazine, trade journals or other writings that your target market is likely to read.

Of all the content marketing strategies, our favorite is writing a book. When you are a published author, you gain considerable credibility, and are viewed as an expert. While it may seem daunting to take the time to write a book and figure out how to write one, we offered some tips on making it easier. You can write a short book (or a series of short books); you can utilize a ghostwriter; and you can download a complimentary copy of the eBook *Write a Book Easily*, which provides a nice roadmap to follow. Just visit the webpage *www.skillbites.net/writeabook* to receive your copy.

If you have questions or we can help you in any way, please feel free to reach out to us. Our contact information is listed on our bio pages. We would appreciate receiving your feedback on this material, and encourage you to share our material with other attorneys.

ABOUT THE AUTHORS:
Judy Weintraub

Judy Weintraub is an attorney with over 30 years legal experience. She runs Weintraub Legal Services, a law firm providing corporate legal services to businesses in the mid-Atlantic region. Ms. Weintraub is also a mediator and arbitrator, serving on the rosters of the American Arbitration Association and the International Institute for Conflict Prevention and Resolution (CPR). And she is the founder and CEO of SkillBites LLC, offering a publishing platform designed specifically for business owners and professionals to get books written quickly and easily.

Connect with Judy:

judy@SkillBites.net

www.SkillBites.net

610-783-4519

Discover other titles by Judy Weintraub at *www.SkillBites.net*:

The Essentials of Negotiating Effectively

How to Build Successful Business Partnerships

ABOUT THE AUTHORS:
Terri Levine

Terri Levine, PhD is the owner of *Terri Levine Worldwide* and is a business and executive coach, and experienced entrepreneur. She assists businesses worldwide with business growth, sales and marketing. She has more than 30 years of business experience, encompassing work with more than 5,000 business owners and entrepreneurs in a variety of industries. She is also a best-selling author and keynote speaker.

Dr. Levine is also the host of the very popular radio Talk Show heard on iHeartRadio (*iheart.com/talk/show/209-The-Terri-Levine-Show*)

The Terri Levine Show: Business Advice You Can Take To the Bank!. She interviews some of the brightest minds in business, sales and marketing today and gets their best tips and tools for the listeners.

Terri's most recent venture is her *Rapid ROI Marketing Model* which combines Terri's passion for helping businesses to grow with her own personal experience gained while building multiple successful business from the ground up.

Learn more at *www.TerriLevine.com*

Contact Terri at *terri@terrilevine.com*

www.ingramcontent.com/pod-product-compliance
Lightning Source LLC
Chambersburg PA
CBHW051252170526
45165CB00004B/1685